REPENT AMERICA, IN THE NAME OF JESUS

The Freedom to Worship for the Christian Church is Threatened

T. H. Logwood

T. H. Logwood

"Thou Shall Not Commit Murder"

T. H. LOGWOOD

Copyright 2019. Second Edition 2020. All Rights Reserved

MURDER IS MURDER

Matthew 5:21 reads, "You have heard that the ancients have told you 'Thou shall not commit murder', and whoever commits murder shall be liable to the courts." Well apparently that is no longer true. As state legislators create new abortion laws, in contradiction to every prior precedence, murder is no longer considered "murder". The blood-sucking lawyers and depraved politicians would have you believe the lie, that abortion is not murder, "it's a liberation of ones alternate consciousness" or some politically correct lunacy. No, wrong! The taking away of life by the hands of another person, by every real life reality, is called murder. The Webster dictionary defines murder as the "unlawful and malicious or premeditated killing of another person". But "the law" says it isn't, or that by some roundabout flowery deception, that "it's okay".

When is the taking of life, whether a fetus, a newborn baby, or another human being, "okay"? The answer is suppose to be "never", it's called murder. The twisting of words and meanings is irrational and insanity at its highest level, and that can not (or should not) be tolerated. How can a nation that cherishes rights and freedoms, then sanctify the killing of its own citizens? How? By laws. By laws, written by crooked lawyers and immoral politicians, and a society that embraces evil as good, is capable of anything they want to do. It is a nation that has fallen away from the moral teachings of its Christian-Judeo foundation, ushering in its own destruction. Is not our babies, conceived or new born, not citizens? Who's next, small children, the elderly, or "Christian Deplorables", that can next be "legally" murdered?

Does anyone remember Nazi Germany and the Holocaust? Or was that erased from the history books also? Under the guise of law, the Fascist (socialist) controlled government made it legal to round up groups of people they disliked, and under "the law", it was legal to kill them. The government sanctioned the murder of their own citizens. Of course, it wasn't called murder; they must have had some legal rationale, which made it acceptable. How many millions of German citizens did their own government murder, by law? Was it 3 million, 6 million?

In America, are we now about 60 million murdered babies (via abortion)! Whether breathing babies or as a fetus, the laws are made to rationalize the murder of its own people. Guess what? Every nation in history that murders its own citizens, by legal decree, does not exist for long. America has allowed this insanity since the key supreme court decision Roe v. Wade in 1973.

Of course, the definition what is life and when it actually begins is a hotly debated issue, and always will be. But, that it beside the point, the taking of another human beings life, premeditated and by law, is still murder. Murder is murder, is it not? More than a moral issue, or a legal debate, it's a political juggernaut. Candidates rise to power, or crumble in obscurity depending which side of the issue they favor. Morality is not the issue, life is not the consideration, but politics rule the evil minded.

Is basic science still taught in schools? Certainly, the godless and immoral politicians have excised God and prayer from the public school system, and also simple biology? When does life begin? It is the most simple and easy answer, immediately. You need a live male sperm, and a live female egg, then when they join, they create a live new being. It doesn't get more simple than that. Debate over. The beginning of life is that simple, a basic biological reality.

This is greatly a political and party issue. Who one stands for

Life or Legalized Death, which candidates support one bill or another. The question of life may well be the key issue in the next election. Should the rights of life, women's rights, family values, or religious morals, be a question of those seeking office? Yes! Absolutely yes, because we are suppose to elect leaders that will protect its citizens. The sole number one priority for the existence of government is firstly and primarily to protect the people they are suppose to govern. The lawyers and deceptive politicians will tell you otherwise, twist the meaning of words, divert your attentions to "free stuff", or the immorality of border walls, or perhaps saving the garden snail. If those are more important topics to you, then vote that way, and keep your fingers crossed that those politicians deliver on their hollow words. Filter through the lies and garbage, and learn what the candidates or leaders have actually done, see how that aligns with your own conscience, then vote. Join with like-minded people and support those candidates. Laws, whether good or bad, right or wrong, depends exactly on whom is elected (by the people).

LIFE IS UNDER ATTACK

America is in trouble, big trouble. From our roots, America was founded as the champion of freedom and liberty, defender of the weak, the protector of the family, especially our children. Have we fallen so far from our blessed beginnings, that now we thirst for the blood of innocents? Where our Christian heritage has given way to liberal and socialistic rituals, now celebrating murder? What in the name and authority of the Lord Jesus Christ is happening in America? Get on your face before Almighty God and beg for mercy. Pray Brethren. Pray without ceasing, right now. We have a heart problem as a nation, it's wicked. God is livid! He will repay the evils now infecting our legal system and state legislatures, and the reality is that His wrath IS coming, and it will be massive.

What has made America different from every other country that has ever existed? Everything! But upon a closer look into the foundations that has made America come into existence at all, is our God. The first settlers came to the New World, primarily escaping religious persecution, to live in a place where they sought the rights and freedom to worship God without the interference from their rulers. Our Founding Fathers framed the miraculous Constitution through God's Spiritual guidance, as this country was borne on the bedrock of divine providence. The young America was based upon Biblical Judeo-Christian truths and principles, and has since grown into the mighty nation it is today. Until recent times, most Americans believed in family, community, hard work, limited government, free expression, reverence for God, Life at conception, individualism, and self-defense. These are traditional American values, and they are gravely threatened.

All that was good and right about America was because the people (the majority of them) were Christians, and tried to follow their lives according to Biblical teachings. America was great, because of our love and reverence for Almighty God. And it has been of our relationship with our Creator, that this country was allowed to grow and prosper. God also has allowed us to be part of His plan for the End Times. America was the one that stood up and recognized the new State of Israel, and has been her staunchest defender. And from that, God has kept this country safe and strong. But that is radically changing.

Roe v. Wade.

Roe versus Wade was a knife into God's heart, and a turning point for America. Sanctioned by the Supreme Court ruling of 1973, the government has allowed the death of our own babies, through the slaughter known as abortion. The legal issue was whether a woman had certain rights over her own body. Rights yes, a woman is a person, and as Americans, we have certain inalienable Rights. The problem is that a "legal right" is different from a "moral right" (or obligation). Just because a law says something is legal to do, doesn't mean that it is a good thing. As morals have fallen off a cliff in America, morality is hardly a consideration any longer.

Abortion is an abhorrence to everything this country founded upon, and contrary to every Judeo-Christian teaching. Yet, these are dark days, signaling that the end is near. How many babies have been killed? Some reports say about 60 million would-be children, have be slain! How in Gods' name has this travesty been allowed to continue? Because our people has turned away from God, and turned to the lusts of this world. This is Satan's world, and since Roe v. Wade, Satan knows his reign of destruction is almost over. And as his control over this world draws to an end, Satan has intensified his thirst for blood and death. And since the

1960's, the sense of morality in this country have collapsed.

One indicator of dwindling moral conviction might be the trend in the marriage-divorce rate. In the 1960's, divorce was about 20%, now over 50% today. The figures are generalized, and without digging into the stats and demographics, but the trend is clear. If divorce rates are in sync with the decline in Christian-Judeo morality, then this makes sense.

In today's humanistic government-dependent society, moral fiber is lacking. This is made ever so clear, as with the recent events . In New York, the legislature has enacted a new abortion law that allows the death of the unborn, up until it draws its first breath! And with glee and the gitty applause of celebration the assembly presented the bill to Governor Como, who cheerfully signed it. What madness is this? Are we back in the days of Canaan, where babies were slain as worship to their pagan gods? And then, the liberal state of Vermont followed suit with a similar law. What fools! Do they not know what they are doing? They are allowing the death of the most innocent and helpless of beings, our own citizens, and sanctioned by legal decree? They want death, and they will have blood upon blood on their wicked hands! God sees this horrid action as open rebellion of His mercy and grace, and the blessings He has bestowed to this land. His wrath will be great! Repent America, God will repay.

And Now Virginia has followed the death-spiral with New York and Vermont. In the hearing before the bill was approved, one of the Virginia Republican House members, a question was asked of Ms. Tran, the Democrat House member that introduced the legislation. They asked her pointedly if she was proposing the abortion option even to the point where the baby was coming out the birth canal. She dodged the question back and forth, until finally affirming, that "yes, the mother can approve the abortion as the baby was coming down the birth canal." The Virginia governor, a doctor himself, also agreed it was the part of the new bill, and the baby would be nicely lain in comfort while the mother and doctors decide to kill the baby. Is this not murder, plain and simple? This is infanticide. Even at the point the baby takes its first breaths of air, they mother and and doctors can kill it?

We are not talking about a fetus a few days or weeks old, but an actual human being, living, and breathing. In every single other case in human existence, killing another human being would be called murder, with grave consequences. But in these three states, murder is now legal. Watch, next it will be legal to kill your child up to age four, or your elderly grandparents, then perhaps your parents. "By law" this is not considered "murder", it may have the politically correct term, like "life liberation", "Honoring the dignity of life", or whatever the blood-sucking lawyers come up with. Murder, by every law, by Gods Word, by every society throughout human existence, murder is murder. Ah, but no longer in the modern "enlightened" liberal secular Satan-worshipping society of the New Babylon.

Remember what many of the Muslim extremists would say about America? "America is the new Satan." They would often rage about the evils of this country, and so on. Hmm, perhaps they are correct after all. If America is no longer the Christian country from its inception, then it must be the pagan-worshiped evil that other groups have touted. They shout, "Death to America", and one day we may see that happen.

For God's people, let this be a battle cry, and a call to arms, for "war is upon us"! And before we can stand against the evil, the Great Satan (as the Muslims call us), we must drop on our faces and pray for forgiveness. For all that still believe in God's sovereignty, His Word, and call yourselves His people, then first we must seek Him. The thing to do is humble yourself in prayer before Almighty God and beg for forgiveness. We have fallen far short in recent decades from the Godly people we once were. And now we must repent and seek His mercy. Before we can fight the evils befalling this nation, we ourselves, in our wicked hearts, must turn to our God for help. Not that any of us are perfect, but for each of us, there are things in our lives that are unclean or have kept us from the intimate relationship with our Lord. And for that, we first must seek his grace through repentant prayer.

GET ACTIVE

Jeremiah 22:3 has this to say to our rulers, "Do justice and righteousness... and do not shed innocent blood". Then in verse 5, the prophet adds, "But if you will not obey these words, I swear by my Myself, declares the Lord, that this house (country) will become a desolation". That is frightening, and true, as we allow our elected leaders to make these unjust and horrid laws. Our best Right and freedom we still have in this country is the vote. As long as the election process remains relatively fair and honest, we can remove the evil politicians, and select better people to uphold our rights and values.

And then, after humbling ourselves in prayer and seeking His face, then ask how best you can make a difference in this war. Join with your brethren in communal prayer; seek out groups and organizations that are standing against the darkness befalling our land. Politically get active and support candidates that abhor abortion, and vote. Letters and phone calls to your elected leaders is important, as well as social media posts, then join with others to spread the disdain for the legalized debauchery. What else can you do? Write a book, like this one! Spread the word, join with like-mind people, and make a difference, we need you!

Support President Trump and those good and Godly cabinet members in his struggle to put this country back on course. Despite the continuous criticism from the biased inflammatory media, President Trump has done many great and positive actions to "make America Great Again", but much more is needed. President Trump loves and supports Life, and has made great strides in protecting and strengthening our religious liberties. He believes in the US Constitution and supports the rights guaranteed therein. He faces firm opposition from nearly every democrat, and some from his own party. His success, and to our benefit, comes from support by favorable members in congress, and from us. Remember that the election is very near, and either we continue to make positive changes under his leadership, or ALL of the positive actions will be reversed if another democrat (socialist) is elected.

THE BIGGER PICTURE

And actually, at stake is far more nefarious than the slaughter of innocents, we are losing our constitutional rights. The bigger picture is the assault of the Rights of Free Speech, the Rights of Worship, the Rights to Assemble, The Rights to Bear Arms, and certainly others are being stripped away with each election. This is true and has been happening more and more. By not voting, or being complacent because you may be displeased with the candidate choices, the other side wins, and is electing poor leaders. If you don't vote, the opposing candidates are winning elections, and many of them want to destroy every constitutional right we have. This is fact, look, read, research, and learn for yourselves what is happening.

And who are being elected. Those gaining political and legal power (to make laws that govern our lives) has been going to liberals, progressives, socialists, and dishonest deceptive politicians, seeking power and riches at the expense of the common man, and in absolute contradiction to our established liberties and freedoms. Many of these folks are democrats, although to be fair, not all democrats adhere to the new party platform. Please don't misunderstand that! There are poor leaders that are republicans and independents as well. Overall, the New Democrat Party is a very different party than what existed before. And because these people are gaining office, they are making laws, some of which are very bad laws.

The latest New York State law that allows death to the people, is a violation of our Rights of Worship, Speech, and the pursuit of happiness, as laid out in the constitution. The deceptive legal establishment will profess the contrary, but they are vicious liars and murders in their own right. We are a nation of laws, and the rule of law is the intent of how the government is suppose to be govern our society. But laws are made that are not always good or right for the people. All abortion laws are legal, but none of them are right. It is by the twisting and perversion of right and wrong by filthy lawyers and crooked politicians that has brought us to this point. It is time to act and do something.

ABORTION IS LEGALIZED MURDER

And what about "the right to life"? The abortion question, is not just a freedom of religious worship, but it is also a freedom of speech. Perhaps the greater overall question is whether it is right and lawful for the government to kill, or sanction the killing, of its own citizens. Although the Supreme Court allowed the ability to kill unborn babies as a rule of law in Roe vs. Wade, is it right? No, it is a disgusting and abhorrence to everything good and honorable that this country touts to be. Murder is murder. An unborn child is still a human being, up until now.

The State of New York and Vermont have passed new laws allowing the death of babies right up until the child takes its first breath. The State of Virginia has now followed their leading. And, the voting assembly members applauded the new law with resounding glee! It is said that liberty will die with resounding applause. Soon, more states will enact laws contrary to tradition and justice. Are we really there? Whether life begins at conception or when a baby draws its first breath is irrelevant. The question is, how can we as a nation allow the murder of our own innocent and defenseless citizens? We are suppose to be a nation ruled by rights protected under the law, but not all laws are good or just. Where is the sanity of our lawmakers and the people? This is murder, plain and simple.

Elections have consequences. You vote for good people to lead us that defend life and liberty, or not. We have seen the definitions of right or wrong changed to suit the desires of elected officials. You vote for your hearts desire, and apparently it's for death. And to have such leaders in power, they will continue to enact laws that will subvert and limit our rights. Just look at all of the regulations and laws that are being passed to limit your liberties. There are many, and more being enacted every day.

Now if the horrid debauchery of killing innocent life is not over-ruled, then the rights of free speech, religious worship, and "the pursuit of happiness", are made mute. Our freedoms as guaranteed under the US Constitution are destroyed. Those lawmakers, supporters of such legislation, and any group or organizations that adheres with such, are murders and co-conspirators. Is this country really going down this path? Then truth and justice in America is a lie!

What follows next? Well, because the murder of babies is made legal, the next step is to broaden that "definition" of whom can be (legally) murdered. Next will be young children no longer wanted by their parents, or perhaps the elderly will be killed at the whim of madmen. Then from there, any opposition group or segment of citizens, like white males, Christians, deplorable republicans, and so on, can face the death squads (by law). The laws can be enacted to do anything one wants, and getting any opposition group out of the way, is equally that simple. "When the sword is unsheathed, it is difficult to put it back without first spilling blood."

Here also, if and when the government is allowed to restrict your rights to own firearms, or takes them away completely, then there will be no more questions about religion, free speech, abortion, rights to assemble, protests against the government, and so on. Those who gain power will abuse it, and then they will oppress the people, which then they will start murdering the citizenry. Strongly ponder these thoughts

AND WHAT TO DO?

As mentioned before, get into a pure and good prayerful time with your God, and beg for mercy and forgiveness. Repent of whatever darkness holds you down, and ask for His help and grace to change your heart. Then give Him praise before you do anything more. Praise is a precursor to prayer, it is in addition to prayer (many say before the actual prayer part), and many pastors and teachers would say that praise is sometimes more important than prayer. Give praise upon the Lord, then prayer for your enemies. Prayers that our leaders making and supporting these evil laws, and the organizations and people also supporting such, have a change of heart. After praying for our enemies, pray for America. Prayers should include for wisdom, guidance, and repentant hearts. Prayers for our "good" leaders, organizations, and others that hold sound doctrine and values. Pray, lots of prayers, and often. Praying is our best and easiest weapon to wield.

Why pray? "We need action! We need to do this, or do that." Yes, perhaps true, but this is not really our fight, it's Gods. We are Gods hands and feet, His voice and light in this dark world. But first we need to pray. Because there is Power in prayer, power by invoking the name of Jesus, and it is through His Spirit, in the spiritual realm, that the real work gets done. Then, go out and do something to share the love of God. Positive changes will come. Do something like meet with like-minded people. Post thoughts and comments on social media. Write a book, letters, and get politically active. There are lots of actions to take, but start with prayer.

MORE ABOUT LOSING OUR LIBERTIES

Is it possible to lose our Constitutional rights and freedoms? These are guaranteed under the law, aren't they? Yes, but no.

With each election, it results in more radical thinking politicians taking office, by which they get laws and regulations passed to silence our religious worship, for instance. Not so long ago, one could pray in school. Now, by laws and restrictions, it takes lawyers and legal battles to be able to meet on a public campus to have a time of prayer. How about courthouses are being stripped of the Ten Commandments, as our laws are based upon. There are groups that are claiming some argument or another, they just want anything Christian removed. How about last Christmas? How many battles did these atheists groups and organizations demanding the end of Christ-mas related everything fight all over the country? There are news stories where anti-Christian groups would set up satanic emblems and decorations next to Nativity scenes. These are all attacks on our constitutional rights of free worship. Apparently to many of these groups, everything is tolerated except Christianity, or anything that invokes the name of Jesus.

Our freedom of speech, part of that 1st Amendment Right, along with Religion, which is also greatly under attack. There more and more laws that restrict what you can say against another person or group. Some of these are "Hate Laws" that also have consequences for speaking adversely. This silencing of open discussion, debate, or defiance, is control of our of free speech. Some politicians seek more control over us by enacting more laws and regulations in every area of our lives. What if you spoke against a government agency or a governmental employee? Laws are being passed to limit what you can say against the government. What was accountability of government by the people, laws are starting to restrict that opposition, and then bring about serious consequences. Censorship is increasing in schools, on social media, certainly throughout the mainstream media. If you are not in lock-step with popular thinking, then you will be shut down.

Learn who the candidates are before you vote. Does the party platform, their set of ideals, align with your own? How do you want to live? Our country is founded on some simple absolute Rights; free speech and freedom to worship are the 1st Rights in the Constitution for a reason. It's important.

Freedom of religious worship? Our Judeo-Christian roots that bore this country and our entire legal system have been greatly under attack as well. We are free to worship whom and what we like, or nothing at all, without the interference of government mandating what we can do. The idea of "separation of Church and State", has been grossly portrayed by those seeking to abolish Christianity. Thomas Jefferson and Hamilton had written about this matter from the beginning, citing that "not" separation, but rather that "government shall not impose a religion". In other words, government would not declare a State religion. Being a person of faith, whatever you believe, and part of the government structure, should not be an issue. It is, and watching every Supreme Court nomination hearing, and even most Cabinet level screenings, there are those people, mostly the democrats, that scream about the separation of Church and State. Having a person that holds a belief and moral compass in public office is a good thing. Look at the corrupt lying filth currently serving in office, and then decide which is better.

If democrat politicians (who have the mission to control the lives of the people) are elected, they will enact more laws to reduce or eliminate the rights and privileges we hold. And in particular our freedom to speak in opposition, our ability to freely worship, our rights to bear arms, and so on. As we lose our freedom of speech (again as an example), we become slaves to the government. And what happens if there is no accountability? Dictatorship. No freedoms, the government becomes all powerful, no opposition, and they hold the sole power of life and death over every citizen. Study history, it's scary.

Don't the republicans seek control also? Yes, sure they do, as all that are elected are subject to the lusts of power and control. It's just that in recent times, the democrat party has become so radical in their quest to control people by restrictive laws and regulations. Is that right or even fair? Some think it's fine, others are less happy, but the movement towards a socialist and totalitarian slavery will end the liberties and freedoms we still have.

This trend in our elections and the types of people elected to office is actually very scary. Too many are pushing for a government-led governmental controlled society. All countries that have embraced that style of slavery are unproductive, with a people that are unhappy. Those nations, historically, have not remained very long.

OTHER FREEDOMS
TO LOSE

Freedom to speak out and speak freely, is not the only right and freedom we can lose, but all of the others as well. The Right to bear arms has been also greatly under seige over the past decade or so.

Gun rights are greatly threatened. The Second Amendment protects the citizens' right to bear arms, for personal and family protection, but also to stand against tyrannical rulers. This fight has escalated in recent years, flamed by the biased media, and outspoken elitists. Here too, the critics claim that having guns is unsafe, yet those individuals have armed security and walled homes. Without the right to defend yourself, do you think the rights of speech or worship will remain? Once the people are disarmed, then the government can become vicious. Study history. Again, recall the rise of Nazi Germany.

We have plenty of good Gun laws in effect, but not adhered to in most states. Rather than add new laws to restrict gun ownership, how about enforce the current laws? For example, the background check laws for gun purchasing was developed with the assistance of the NRA. The way it is suppose to work, is that criminal offenders are suppose to have their names and information submitted by the state and local levels into the NCIC database (the National Crime Information Center). From there, those with access to the system can then approve or deny a purchase via the information submitted. Therein lies the rub, information has to be submitted into the system, which is done at the state or and local levels. Not to do so, makes the whole background checking system incomplete due to the lack of relevant data. It is a good law and a good system, if it were used as intended.

Also, beware the "Red Hat" laws. Many states are implementing what is called Red Hat laws, whereby any person can simply accuse another person of being "dangerous". This then triggers law enforcement to confiscate the accused persons' firearms. Based merely on hearsay, without proof, and without due process, ones firearms can be seized. Is that not a violation of many of our personal rights and freedoms? Yes, and it is yet another way the leftists are starting to "void" the Second Amendment. The second amendment is a tough fight to try and abolish. But anti-gun activists just have to get more regulations, taxes, and restrictive laws in place to make gun ownership very difficult.

Like every issue the leftists scream about, they hold themselves above the law, and often not adhering to their own arguments. These democrat and others are hypocrites seeking their the own agendas. Many of these outspoken politicians and anti-gun activists have their own security guards.

As you look at the history of every nation that has turned socialist, the first thing the government would do is to remove the guns. Remove the ability of the citizens to fight against injustice, and the people will be easily controlled. Remove the guns, and all other rights and freedoms can not be defended. Again, take Nazi Germany for example. There was strong active opposition to the rise of the national-socialists, but once the guns were seized, the Nazis eliminated all of the critics. And we are talking about the government killing its own citizens. America is moving closer to this type of government. It is that scary.

How about the Rights to Assemble? Could meeting at church be met with armed police or death squads? Not yet in America, but many places around the world, yes! Christian persecution is literally a life or death struggle in many countries. That can happen here too! Elect leaders hostile to the Christian faith, and watch what happens. Previously, there was a law (the Johnson Amendment) whereby the preacher could not talk about politics or governmental actions in the pulpit. That has been removed, thanks to President Trump, so the truth and even of politics can be talked about openly. That can change back again just as easily.

THE HEALTH CARE ISSUE

Although not a right or freedom per se, it is a topic that relates to the laws revolving around abortion. Women's rights groups, Planned Parenthood, many politicians, and socialist elitists are trying to push their agendas as part of the health care issue. Women have different needs than men, that is a biological fact, and should not include the fluid gender dysphoria popularized by the left. Women are women, and have special medical needs and concerns, that men can not fully comprehend. By God's design, women are the ones that bear life. Women probably have more, certainly different, health needs than men.

By politics and the laws of insanity, those groups, like Planned Parenthood, say that a woman even giving birth, should have the say whether to murder the baby. They argue about rights, a woman's right to choose, and all sorts of ludicrous arguments. And the laws are such that the doctor, and supposedly doctors, then determines the life or death outcome. Are such procedures then allowed under the various health insurance programs? They will be under a "universal health care" system, like the former Obama Care (the Affordable Care Act). A free market approach to health care would make abortion services a policy option, versus a government mandate that everyone pays covers. Again, it is the people we elect that will design and enact the laws.

What about private insurance plans versus tax-payer funded public programs like medi-care? Do I have the say where and how my tax dollars can or should be used for health care coverage? Again, it's about voting and electing leaders to design laws to allow or deny various medical procedures. It is about money, power, and control, who has it, and who is trying to get it. The victims are the women, our freedom of choice, and society as a whole.

The socialist medical programs enacted by Obama were not only unconstitutional, but it promoted abortion, and other immoral practices. The one-payer system, that Obama Care was trying to implement, was that government would control it, and therefore a crucial part of our lives. It took tax dollars from every person, to pay for things like abortion, which is wealth redistribution, and contrary to conscience of unwilling citizens. It was a terrible and costly debacle, infringing on our rights of religious worship and beliefs, and enforced by government imposed penalties and the overtly powerful IRS.

The Party "Not" for the People, or Life

The new democrat party promotes an "open door" stance in regards to borders and immigration, government oversight of religious values, control of education, a government sponsored health care system, highly restrictive gun ownership (if not outright confiscation), and a crackdown on freedom of expression. They encourage government programs to take care of every need, including income equality. They elevate the status of illegal immigrants, including the criminals and child-slavery bondsmen, over legal and natural borne American citizens. Life of the unborn has no rights, according to democrat dogma. The new party promises higher wages via the redistribution of wealth, by taxing the evil rich (white) aristocracy. Is this what people want from their governing bodies?

The radical wing uses slogans and bold words to promote their beliefs. "Be tolerant of other people and their lifestyles." "Save the planet by ending fossil fuels." "The government is your family, your provider, and your god." The bottom line is, they want a government controlled socialist State. The decisions and policies for the people, made by an elite group of "honorable and intelligent" leaders, as they know best how to govern the lives of people. They promise the "good life", without the worry of consequence. Research and learn for yourself, who and what the new democrat party really stands for, but they do not stand up for Christian values.

Wake up Brethren. Wake up America. This is happening. Over the past several decades or so, we have seen so many traditions and what we would call Christian values being eroded. Look at marriage for instance. In the 1940s and 50s, divorce was not very common. Now, at least half of all people have been divorced at least once! Socialistic teachings, human-centered, Sensitivity (or tolerance) training, are forces seeking to sway voters into this "progressive thinking". Anything to take the focus off of Christianity, and the world value system has eroded every traditional norm. The erosion of everything America once was is very real, and about to sink this nation. It is said by many pastors, "we are one generation away from losing Christianity in this country. It's true, look at church attendance. Most churches are nearly empty, and the few that attend, are mostly older folks. Youth, some, but not many. Sports and entertainment venues are packed, but the churches are empty and closing. Total erosion of this country's' foundation is real.

POLITICAL PARTIES - FLIPPING RED TO BLUE

The new democrat party aligns itself to bold speech with no substance. The party for the people is no more. The new party uses violence, "hate speech", and divisive rhetoric to stir up the masses of brainwashed zombies to overthrow society, on every issue of tradition, law, and freedoms. The new party professes the goodness of socialistic ideals, no support for the rights of life, but white-washes the realities of repeated historical failures. Condemnation without solution. The "Peoples Party" is no longer the party of the people, but by Elitists pushing to overturn the rights of free speech, worship, the rule of law, and equality for all. They are indoctrinating of our school children with the ideas that "government provides", versus hard work, family tradition, and merit through achievement.

This radical departure of traditional norms relates exactly to every election, where more and more districts and States are turning "blue". Turning blue, or democrat, was not a bad thing, but the Kennedy-era Democrat, the working man's party, is long gone. The general populace is being brainwashed by empty promises that touts restriction and control, unsubstantiated opinion over logic and reason. Yet the vote turns blue, more often and in more counties and states. It's like in the movies, when the people change from normal to zombies, and the power of the individual is given over to a deadened brainwashed mass hysteria.

If this country is to be changed, let it be changed, through the process of law as it was founded. But what is changed, may not be what is good or right, or fair. And what changes, is not easily changed back. If traditions are deemed wrong, and what we have previously known as failed ideologies become entrenched, then individual liberties are restricted. The new rule of laws becomes contrary to those established by our forefathers, and that seems to embrace evil over what we used to call good. And as power becomes concentrated in the hands of a few, there is no freedom of worship, freedom of speech, or anything else.

Who, or what groups adhere to what you hold as good and right? What you believe in, and the rights and privileges you enjoy, are just a few votes away from being changed. Think for yourself, and decide in the way that works best for you. Align yourself with those that hold those principles and ideals you want. And of course, pray. Pray for wisdom.

THE ELECTION OF CALIFORNICATION

Just because what was, should never imply that something will remain. Pride or delusion can be a strong drink, but the truths and realities of this world have a sneaky way of catching even the best of people off guard. The results of the 2018 midterm elections was alarming from the perspective that democrat turnout was very high. The democrat Blue Wave, as it was called in the media, was successful in winning many more races than they should have. They won, or nearly won, as in many races, not because of the merits and experiences of the candidates, but rather from the marketing campaign that promoted them.

Traditional influences on voters, like jobs, economy, family, or faith, are no longer the driving principles that many voter segments care about anymore. If so, with the great economic rebound, and the successes President Trump has had (despite the media lies), one would forecast that republicans should have won by vast margins in 2018. That was just not so, the wins were marginal at best. Depending on the voter groups or segments, they care about different optics. Whether it is of hyped rhetoric, or emotional dribble and fear, many groups vote based on superficial perceptions. Facts and realities don't assure votes any longer. Younger people are especially swayed by promises of "free stuff", free education, and emotional topics like saving the planet.

Now what is so wrong and bad about Democrat Blue? "That is a biased and 'racist' statement. Only a dumb religious fanatic redneck would say such things, obviously they are degenerate deplorable republicans." What difference does it make if a county or state is Blue or Red, democrat or republican, that's just politics. At the end of the day, people are just trying to get through the day, free to do their own thing. Who should care which political party is in office, it has nothing to do with daily life. What? Who should care? All of us.

That is the whole point, it makes All the difference! It makes a difference who leads us. The values and principles our leaders have, and how every aspect of our daily lives is influenced by governmental policy and laws. All of that matters to Christians and most Americans. To what point can or should government dictate what "we the people" should, do, think, or act? How is it, that a select group of leaders, rule over how we regulate our family values and beliefs? How can our elected leaders cower to the arm-twisting tactics of radical anti-life, anti-family groups like Planned Parenthood, to Antifa and the Black Lives movement, that uses public taxpayer money to lobby and bribe politicians to enact abortion laws? Because we are not standing up and getting our votes cast. We are not joining with other people and groups to support candidates and sound values. If we don't like the laws, we need to elect leaders that hold to more sound principles.

A BLUE AMERICA

The end game is this; a democrat controlled Washington, forever. The new democrat platform values government-sponsored, government-influenced, government control, of every aspect of American life, including reproduction and what a woman can or can not do with her body. In other words, a socialist America.

The current democrat party is wrought with socialist ideals of government dependence and influence over the masses. The few Kennedy-era Democrats who are left in the party, are dead silent. There are moderate and conservative democrats. There are many good and decent Democrats who are pro-life. Does anyone ever hear a peep from them? Their party won't allow them to voice any dissenting opinion, and the fake news media never shows any of them. Those good honorable people are puppets of the radical left wing of the party. Do we want them to regain power in Washington?

Again, recall the Obama era. Eight years of governmental regulations, weak and decimated business and economic freefall, increasing taxes that drained your hard-earned resources, government failure to provide the promised health care, weak and disrespected influence worldwide, and division between the diverse peoples that make up America. Remember how the democrat leadership was anti-Christian and anti-Israel? Look at the Johnson Law (if that's correct) where a pastor could not speak out about politics or politicians in the pulpit. Isn't that a violation of our 1st Amendment rights? Exactly as mentioned earlier, but it was in fact happening. The Obama era, was a leftist, near socialistic government that was moving to void every right and freedom we are suppose to have. This is just a foreshadow of the things to come, if we the people don't get active and elect good leaders. Compare then to now.

Rather than assess or describe a candidate, look at their records of how they have handled the affairs of the people. How do each of the democrats (and republicans); deal with the economy and taxes, national sovereignty, and protection of the citizens. How well did each handle health care, education, immigration and borders, protecting the rights and freedoms guaranteed under the Constitution? What was or is their stance in regards to church, life, and abortion? Of those principles that you value, how did each of these candidates fare? These are questions that should be asked at every election, for every candidate, regardless of party affiliation.

The Clinton era started a downward spiral of the democrat party. With each successive candidate and leader, the party platform, their principles have moved further and further away from mainstream democrats, and most Americans. With every scandal, corruption, and dirty laundry exposed, it has turned away the masses of would-be democrat supporters; hence they supported Trump in 2016. Certainly, this may be greatly generalized, but to the average voter, Christian, republican, or conservative, or other, the democrat party has greatly changed, and not for the better.

Voters can be swayed and convinced by the barrage of media and promises that candidates spew. With the Kennedy-era generation gone, now the Millennials, the Generation-X, the younger voters, are easily bamboozled by social media hype and fake biased news. The younger voter blocks are influenced by less than traditional values, and education indoctrination by social activist teachers. Are they moved by candidate policies or promises? Perhaps they are more interested in the "feelings" and superficial things like the promises for "freebies' that gets their attention. "Kudos" to the democrat party voter outreach program, it has been very successful in mass marketing. They reach out and follow up on interested voter prospects far better than any republican machine.

And the republican base is getting old. The ol' reliable republican base is changing, getting beyond voting age or ability, with poor outreach to the younger generation, or the new citizen bases. The republican public image is that of old tired white men, supported by big business, and the pursuit of wealth. Family values and tradition doesn't register with the younger voters, especially as the decline in marital commitments continues to plummet, leaving disenfranchised families. The younger generations are more tolerant of anything other than restrictive Christian churchy dogma. And a biased media deflates any positives that republican leaders make, and exonerates the new democrat values over truth and impartiality.

WHAT TYPE OF LEADERS?

Who we elect, will result in laws by lawmakers, like those in New York, Vermont, and Virginia. The 2018 mid-term elections was wrought with manipulation and deceit, with the backing of main stream media, and powerful wealthy donors. The democrats were using Gestapo-like tactics to quell any resistance, twisting the truths and news, and used the "mob" to intimidate and harass opposition. This is not the Democratic Party of JFK or even Bill Clinton. What was the welfare of the working man under the Kennedy era Democrats, which was the cornerstone of the party, has given way to radical socialistic doctrine, with legions of brainwashed stooges to carry out mob violence and endless protests. Rather than come up with solutions to fix an issue, or to make lives better for the people, they use rhetoric and hate speech, and the double standard to advance a dark agenda. That had in fact prompted the newly elected house legislatures in New York to design and pass such horrid abortion laws. Hey, as noted, elections have consequences, and if people don't get out there to vote, this is what happens.

For example, President Trump and the border wall. The will of the people that elected Trump, want a border wall and increased national security. It is fact that large amounts of drugs, crime, slavery, and masses of invading people, come across the southern border, half of which is in Texas. Most Americans want this invasiveness to end. America is a sovereign nation that has the right to have a border, and restrict people and activities from entering the country. This is also factual, and mandated in the US Constitution that the president has the right and authority to protect and enforce our national borders from outside influences.

Bill Clinton argued and demanded for a wall as protection along the border. So did Obama. Pelosi, Schumer, Ms. Clinton, and many other democrats, as shown on numerous video clips. Each cited the needs for border walls and security. Yet, because Trump is so greatly hated by most of the democrat leadership, the media, and their brain-washed stooges, they all now oppose border security. For President Trump to succeed on this key election issue, the democrats would suffer greatly. Therefore, despite protecting Americans, our rights, our safety, they will oppose the wall until election day.

On and on, there seems to be examples of prominent party leaders that profess one thing, yet do the opposite. Too many of them make promises, only to deny such upon gaining office. Granted, politics is an ugly business sometimes, and some candidates and elected people are morally corrupt, but that seems to be normal in this day and time in which we live. The latest opinion polls suggests that President Trump has an approval rating of about 40 to 45%, and Congress about 12 to 14%. Whether accurate or not, the fact is that many people don't trust or like our elected leaders. Then vote them out. Learn about the candidates before they get into office, and join with those that are like-minded. Use your rights and freedoms to assemble, speak up, and then vote.

BEWARE THE BLUE HATS

To be clear, if the new democrat party holds to the teachings and practices of socialistic ideals, then decide if electing those candidates aligns with your own values. What the democrat leaders want is power and control. They have, and will, beat down all opposition to that end, and that would not benefit Christians, or America.

Remember what Machiavelli said back around 1500, "Power corrupts, and absolute power corrupts absolutely". And examining history, even recent history, this is exactly true. When leaders get into power, unchecked by laws and constitutional limitations, then the mischief that resides in a mans' heart, festers into evil. Power is a drug, and intoxication that drives leaders mad, and ruins nations. The victims are the citizens. It is said that if a government is allowed to gain power (unchecked), then those leaders first abuse the power to their own gain. Then they oppress the people and silence opposition, and then, by historical fact, they mass murder their citizens. And it starts with the babies.

"That can't happen in America. We have laws. We have three branches of government to limit power, and we only elect good honest leaders." Too many people have become brain-washed to the euphoria of promises made by candidates and elected leaders. Too many people have forgotten God, to take responsibility for their own actions, and can no longer can discern right from wrong. The liberals have screamed Christianity out from our schools, beaten down anything relating to the name of Jesus in public, and every facet of our lives is about fear of offending somebody or some group. Stop it! Stand up and fight for what you believe in, because it's slipping away. "Don't talk about abortion, it might hurt somebody's feelings." Oh how sad, what about the babies feelings? Pretty difficult to have feelings when the doctors are murdering them. Stop it with the "touchy feely feel-good movement" that political correctness mandates. That is a socialist trick, to make everyone think they should be treated equally, feel the same, earn the same, be the same type of robot. Easier to control people that way, and it is done through laws.

As leaders are elected, they push laws and regulations to favor groups or individuals, or other self-serving ends that can limit rights and privileges previously held. Elected leaders can fill the judicial branches with like-mind judges to twist or limit laws. Politicians can band together to halt or limit the good works and laws that are suppose to govern the nation. Our constitutional government is a fragile system, threatened when corrupt leaders gain power.

Over the past number of decades, individual rights and liberties have been greatly smeared. Look at the Freedom of Speech (and Religion), and the Right to Bear Arms. Those two areas have been radically limited, and far from the Framers original intent. If the right to bear arms is further degraded to the point where we can no longer protect ourselves and family, and, the ability to stand against a tyrannical government, then all other rights and freedoms will be lost. It is the right to protect yourself with firearms that assures we have all the other rights and freedoms will be protected. Take that away, by legal limitations, then beware the "Death Squads".

The Nazis were a great lesson in socialism and the brainwashing of the people. They were socialists with a national theme. They came to power in a time of crisis, offering promises and protection. "The more you help us fix and change the laws, the more we can provide for your needs". Laws changed, power consolidated, to the point where the private ownership of guns was banned. Guns for personal protection were outlawed and taken from the people. Without the ability to protect yourself or stand against unjust rulers, freedoms of speech and religious practices were taken away from the people. More and more rights and freedoms were given up or taken away, to the point where Hitler became all powerful, pushing his personal agenda onto the nation and the world. How did that turn out for their citizens? How many millions, of their own citizens, did the government slaughter? Remember World War II, it was the result of corrupt leaders in power? Is the war still taught in our school system, or was it removed because it might offend somebody?

Along the same progression and results, the Russians under Stalin murdered millions and millions of their own citizens who opposed his gain of power. The same scenario as with Nazi Germany. A nation of laws, rights, and liberties, whittled away by leaders, then consolidating their power as given (or taken), to the death of the people, and ruin of the nation. Remember the tolerant society of the Soviet Union? How about peaceful friendly China?

Not much is ever talked about Cambodia. Paul Pott, and the "Hitler youth-like Red Shirts", enforcing the dictates of evil leadership, to the death of millions of peaceful citizens. Recall the grim stories of the killing fields? In every country, throughout Africa, South America, and Asia, where power is allowed to concentrate into the hands of a few rulers, abuse, oppression, and death follows. Every time, without fail, just study history. That is, if the history books are not re-written or burned to hide the truth. Beware, because history has a nasty way of repeating itself to the unwary.

The notion that socialism is "okay" or even good for a nation is absurd. It does not work, never has, never will. It can not, because "power corrupts, and absolute power corrupts absolutely". It has turned out disastrously for every nation since the dawn of man, and no rational way it can ever change. Human nature is that of violence and a thirst for power. And when there is no longer in morale compass that is religiously based, then morality that is right or wrong, becomes based on "Human Relativism". There is no right, no wrong, everybody is free to think what they want. "My reality and what I believe is right or wrong, is different than your reality." Well, when the government says, that its ok to kill babies coming out of the birth canal, and that it's the right of the mother and her doctors, then that is a country nearing total destruction. Then it will be, that the lawyers and leaders will make the laws to justify killing older children, the elderly, and "those racist Christians always pushing their morality, it hurts my feelings". Our babies are being slaughtered today, and the Christians will be persecuted tomorrow. Who would have ever guessed that America would sink so low?

The difference with now, and our governmental structure, is God. America was founded with a Judeo-Christian belief, becoming the foundational stones of every law and thought written in the US Constitution. The leftists and educational elitists will deny that, and scream about some insane alternate reality, but fact is fact. They are working diligently to change the books and the facts, to hide these truths. If libraries still exist where books (the kind with ink and paper) still reside, one can research the writings of every founding father and framer of the document to read of their faith-based ideology. Is that a bad thing? The leftists of the democrat party would say so, because their agenda is very different.

America has lasted for over two hundred years, with the ideas that individuals are good if not oppressed by their rulers, and that man can do good works. Look at what America has done, created, built, fought for, stood against, the freedoms and liberties enjoyed, and so on. There are a lot of negative things that has happened over this time also. True, but the system of this government, for people to rise up and make positive changes for all, has prevailed. The American system of government, built on our religious premise, has worked for the health and happiness of all (or most anyways). The American system of representative government is not perfect. We are flawed people, and sometimes we mess up. We can be greedy, hateful, self-servicing, and so on, but the government was designed to balance the concentration of powers, which has worked well until recently.

Our system of government, guarantees the rights and privileges of the individual is protected. We have the freedom to speak out against the government, and someone who wails against the goodness of our country, is also protected. Why change this? Why would any rational sober person think there is a better system to govern a nation? Apparently, there many and organizations that see it differently.

A COUPLE FINAL THOUGHTS

If democrat politicians (who have the mission to control the lives of the people) are elected, they will enact laws to reduce or eliminate the rights and privileges we hold. In particular, our freedom to worship God as we like, the ability speak in opposition of the government or laws that are enacted, our rights to join together in public or private, are all gravely at risk. As we lose our freedom of speech (again as an example), we become slaves to the government. Power and control unchecked, will destroy a nation. Killing the most innocent and precious of God's creation, our babies, He will repay in kind, and destroy this nation. God will not be mocked, even if cleverly worded in a legal document.

Don't the republicans seek control also? Yes, sure they do, as are all elected officials are subject to the lusts of power and control. It is just that in recent decades, the democrat party has become so radical in their quest to control people through restrictive laws and regulations. Is that right or even fair? Some think it's fine, others are less happy, but the movement towards a socialist and totalitarian slavery will end all of the liberties and freedoms we still have.

This trend in our elections and the types of people elected to office is actually very scary. Too many candidates, elitists, organizations, and segments of the population are pushing for a government-led, governmental-controlled society. Free health care, free schooling, abortion on demand, all have great costs. Nothing is free. It comes from high taxation rates of the working man, but also through the limitations imposed on our freedoms to make choice and decisions.

Our system of government was designed and set up to assure the people would have the liberty to become all they can aspire to do (if not murdered at birth). The freedom of free and open speech, and religious liberties, have been the cornerstone of this country, rooted in the process of free and open elections. Every vote counts, and every citizen has a duty to make this country better, according to their own conscience.

As our society writhes with turmoil of the legality of life, the 2020 election cycle is heating up as it approaches election day. Many groups are seeking to undermine our rights and liberties to vote, to have free and open speech, our rights to worship, and the rights afforded to life. It is critical for the survival of the nation as a whole; to learn about the candidates and what they value, and stand with those who think the same. This is no time for professing Christians or any American to sit idle, there is just too much at stake.

And lastly, keep in mind what Gods word tells us, repent; turn away from what we are doing. There are many scriptures that continually repeat this, like from Zechariah 1:3 and 4, in part reads, "...Thus says the Lord of hosts, 'Return to Me' declares the Lord of Hosts." "...Return now from your evil ways and from your evil deeds". Not to do so, invites the wrath that is coming to this country. May the Lord be with you, and all of us.

ABOUT THE AUTHOR

I grew up in a middle class family, had a father that worked, a mother that stayed home and raised children, the typical traditional American home. We had a small house, one car, (no) white picket fence, we had pets, regular schooling, church-goers, watched news and various TV shows, and had all of the cliche normal things in life typified during the 1950s and 60s. Life was normal and decent, reasonably peaceful, and safe.

My father was a veteran, worked a blue collar job, and was a straight-line democrat, just like his father before him. The Kennedy era thinking of party politics was pretty much his thinking as well. And for many decades, that seemed to work well in America. I too learned and adopted similar ideas of how life and government should work and coexist.

But that has changed radically over the past couple decades, as the democrat party is no longer the party of the average working man. One would best describe the party as what we used to call the Communist-Socialist party during that earlier era. Now the party is all about hate speech, bigotry, division, dirty-politics, rampant dishonesty and deception by party leaders and candidates, and everything revolving around government control. This is no longer the democrat party America once loved.

The candidates and false narratives they promoted were enough to make me switch to the Republican Party. Over the last many election cycles while the democrats drove further left, I pushed my family and friends to switch parties and vote further right. Not that the republicans are perfect by any means, but they do hold to more of the values and principles I do. The biggest area where they align with my own thinking are the ideas of limited government, the sanctity of life, and support for the Constitution. Upholding our rights and freedoms are more their forte, so this is where we will stay.

My hope is to share these thoughts with you, so that you can glean some insight of the struggle we face over our dying liberties. Thank you reading this.

Also consider these other books written about our Rights and Freedoms. These also are found on Amazon Kindle under the Politics section. Look for:

"The Democrat Blue Wave is the Zombie Apocalypse"
by T. H. Logwood
ASIN: B07MYBFKT1

* * * * *

"Don't Tread on Me"
By T. H. Logwood
ASIN: B07X5DRRYB

* * * * *

"The End of American Liberty"
by T. H. Logwood
ASIN: B07HPYZWTF

* * * * *

"The Democrat Blue Wave is the Texas 2nd Alamo"
by T. H. Logwood
ASIN: B07N7N2WG6

* * * * *

"The End of American Freedom"

by T. H. Logwood
ASIN: B07MSJ4QD7

* * * * *

"The U.S.S. La Porte (APA 151), The Pearl of the Pacific"
by T. H. Logwood
ASIN: B07L6JXRB9

* * * * *

"A Walk in the Sub-Alpine Meadows: A Look at the Tuoloume
Meadows Ecosystem"
by T. H. Logwood
ASIN: B07HM928TH

* * * * *

"Collecting Old Stock Certificates: A Look at the Past"
by T. H. Logwood
ASIN: B07HNX1FGK